PHYLLIS DILLER
HOW TO BE

Vol. 02

Maija Di Giorgio

PHYLLIS DILLER
HOW TO BE

Copyright 2013 Hollywood Outlaws, LLC.

Dedicated to the
memory of the legendary
Phyllis Diller

Acknowledgements

Thank you to everyone who helped make this interview and book possible: Ronald and Sylvia Di Giorgio, Heather McConnell, Biagio Tripodi, Pamela Green, Karin Slote, Rain Pryor, Tony Martinelli, Lisa Collins, William J. Roche, Marlene Copeland, Joan Copeland, Melissa Copeland, Richard David Copeland, Ninon Petrella, Ninon Petrella, Matthew Copeland, Al Barone, Lynn, Miranda and Michael Cirillo, Richard and Nancy McConnell, Mimma Pereira...and of course my little Giuseppe.

Preface

We had no idea that Phyllis Diller would be one of the most remarkable women any of us would ever meet. She had a presence unlike anyone else. At the time, she was in her early eighties and had more exuberance than anyone a quarter of her age. I think her jewelry may have weighed more than she did, and to say she looked absolutely fabulous, is an understatement. And, all of that was determined in the first five minutes of meeting her.

In the interview with Maija, Ms. Diller was completely captivating. Her one of a kind laugh rolled through the entire interview. She shared wisdom that could only be gained from a consummate comedic artist such as herself with a wide breadth of experiences in many art forms with many other great artists. This interview truly incapsulates the theme of How To Be. Anyone reading this, artist or not, has the opportunity to gain powerful knowledge that would help him in life and any chosen career path. The entire crew feels blessed to have been granted this interview and to have spent time in the presence of a such a great woman and great artist. Phyllis Diller's contribution to the world of comedy will be missed but never forgotten.

-Heather McConnell

A Note from Maija

I will always remember the day I met Phyllis Diller. In just one conversation, she taught me so much about comedy, and at the same time gave me hope that my life and my career could and would improve. Of course, I did not do my homework before meeting her face to face, so in my back pocket I had only my fondest childhood memories of watching her guest appearances on *Scooby-Doo and Croft Superstar*. I would quickly realize the impact Ms. Diller had made on the movement of women in business, but it would be years before I would fully understand all of the wisdom she was sharing.

At the time of this interview, I didn't seem to understand that thinking of myself as a person before I thought of myself as a female would cause such hardships. As I have grown older, I have come to understand the labels that go with my gender. There are many bruised egos that I leave behind me and many more that seem to throw themselves in front of me, attempting to block my journey towards my success. As I try to navigate my path around them by constantly redefining myself, communicating, and rerouting my path to becoming the person I want to be, I see the bruised egos stacking higher. I constantly think, "Maybe it just can't be done. Maybe they are right. Maybe I am just crazy. I'm too old. And I'm a woman." Then I think of my lesson in life from a sit down with Phyllis Diller. Here was a woman who turned to comedy as a means to feed her 4 children. Who didn't even start her craft till she was in her late 30s. Who not only didn't have a life partner, but redefined the very craft of comedy because she didn't have a stand-up partner. Phyllis Diller was the only one in her circle as the stand alone stand-up. And at a time when women were forbidden to own property, she held her own on the mic, in life and for her family. How many male egos and straight out "no's" did she have to face? So I pick myself up, dust myself off and think of my Phyllis Diller interview. A wise lesson in the craft of comedy, and a profound and cathartic lesson on life.

Side Note:

On the way to the interview I am sure there was a crazy debacle of my "producer"...(and I use the term lightly because my father actually paid to produce the film) throwing a verbally abusive attack on me and my crew, while insisting we needed a manly representation to make this film happen but I no longer remember it. I put up with the ego-maniacal nonsense because meeting the comedy greats day after day was like walking around in a Willy Wonka factory.

I also don't remember much of what happened before this interview because Ms. Diller's energy was so calm, loving and intense that it warded off every anxiety and negative energy that I was surrounded by. In fact, it didn't even ward it off, it totally neutralized it. She gave us a tour of the Los Angeles Friars Club in Beverly Hills which is no longer in existence. It was a dream being in the heart of comedy history and sitting with this powerful woman who was 2 years shy from 90 at the time. I will tell you one thing… if I never reach the goal of my journey, I have certainly had many moments of gold on it. This is one of those moments for me….my time with Phyllis Diller.

Maija:	I'm a comedian, out of New York. And…
Phyllis:	You work as a Comedian?
Maija:	I work as a stand-up. And we've been doing this project.
Phyllis:	Give me your last name again.
Maija:	DiGiorgio. Very complicated. There are too many vowals and too many 'i's and 'j's . And we've been doing this project on comedy because I think comedy has changed. I don't think it's changed for the better. Especially as I'm learning to create, I'm keeping up and I'm digging myself in the hole and the material that isn't…. I think the right type of material that people are doing today.
Phyllis:	You think? You believe that?
Maija:	Yeah, with a lot of the comics… I see a lot of it. It's just a lot of trash on TV.
Phyllis:	You work clean?
Maija:	I work clean.
Phyllis:	In the long run you'll win. No doubt about it.
Maija:	That's why I'm a tremendous fan of yours. As I keep looking and researching more, we are doing this project with Richard Belzer, and I had no idea. The more I researched about how incredible you are. Because we are sitting with the woman who is – I don't know if you guys

know this – But she is not only a comedian, but an author and a gourmet chef. And a mother of 5 and a concert pianist who has played all over the country – I don't know- all over the world. And started this..I understand at 37 years old.

Phyllis: Yes, at 37. You aren't 37 yet.

Maija: No. And with 5 children to raise. That's…. and at the time period. I think it's difficult now. I know that I spend time. Could you tell me, how did you have the courage to do these things?

Phyllis: Well, I was terribly motivated, as you know. If you threatened, a … say a lion mother in the jungle, who has cubs, you're dead meat. In other words, I had that kind of motivation. I had to feed these cubs, and it was up to me to make a living. And since I chose comedy, that was what I was going to do with- my instrument would become comedy. Fortunately, I have a great sense of humor. Therefore, it was possible. With that kind of motivation it would have taken an awful lot to stop me.

Maija: How many women were doing stand-up when you first started?

Phyllis: Not- nobody was doing my kind of stand-up. In fact when you say stand-up, you usually mean a single person, working alone. Even the men were working double. Martin and Lewis and all these others, everybody was working double. So, it made it even more powerful for me because not only was I a woman, but I was actually doing it alone.

Maija: That's incredible! So you're one of the first...

Phyllis: Because it was Burns and Carlin and everybody was doing a duo and, you know, that's easier. When you are doing it all by yourself, you are responsible for all the material.

Maija: So, what was it like for the first time when you went on stage?

Phyllis: Terrifying! Totally terrifying! Totally terrifying! We're talking flops. And, you know, when the first time you really are, you aren't a seasoned performer and you really aren't that good, your material isn't that good, you haven't had the experience. You need experience.

Maija: Well, I understand that you did well because from what I have heard, was that your first booking lead to 96 or 97 weeks?

Phyllis: It led to permanency. In other words, they believed in me. That was it, and I believe they believed in me because I believed in me. Belief in yourself is one of your major necessities and never waver with that belief because it

	weakens you. If you have a doubt ever, a little teeny doubt, it weakens you. Then you aren't as powerful.
Maija:	That's incredible. So, where did you…..did you always know that you wanted to go into comedy and were just a mother and taking care of your kids and just know?
Phyllis:	Actually, I started out in my youth to become a musician, and I might just add at this point that most comics are musicians. The list is so long of famous comics who are truly musicians. Jack Benny with the violin and Henny Youngman with his violin….the cello of…..what was his name… I forget…anyway. Johnny Carson, the drummer
Maija:	Really?
Phyllis:	Yes! A fine drummer. Sid Caeser made a living playing saxophone. Phil Silvers, famous clarinet player. I mean the list is endless. So, you see, comedy is something to do with the ear. It's an audio art. So, that's where music comes in. That's why comics make wonderful actors because they actually listen and hear and, of course, rhythm. Oh my god! Timing, you know that ol'… It's almost a cliche'. Timing is everything. And musicians know that, that's part of music.
Maija:	Now, what was your first film project that you worked on?
Phyllis:	Oh, well. It was a famous movie which holds up today with Warren Beatty and Natalie

Wood, *Splendor In the Grass*, Elia Kazan was the director. And they talk about starting at the top- a classic movie. But I had a walk-on, a bit part. Played Texas Guinan. What a thrill to even watch the process of a big scene being done. There were like 200 extras in that scene and it was a night club scene, and it took 2 days to shoot just a few minutes because, you see, when you are working with that many extras, "You stand here, You stand there". Oh my God! Please.

Maija: And where did you go from there?

Phyllis: Umm. Just kept plodding. Plodding, plodding, plodding. Plodding and plotting. Plodding and plotting. Always thinking about what's the next level. Always trying to get to the next level. After all the clubs and unimportant gigs, as we say. The next level was better television shows, bigger television shows, and hotel rooms. In those days, in the days when I was working, one of the top levels of our business was to get into the fine hotels, you know. The fine rooms, the empire rooms and always looking. And here in Hollywood, you know, stand-up comics always are headed for their own television shows. Like Seinfeld. Cristopher Titus and all the guys. The next level here is television and then the next level is movies!

Maija: What do you think of those differences, the changes in stand-up that you have seen. Working towards television is different in a way that you think that makes it better or do you think it is damaging to the art?

Phyllis: Well, I think it's always good to have another goal. A higher goal. Because you see it, it expands your work. You have to be better. So, you should always be striving. Once you get comfy, then you are no longer working and striving. It's pretty much static and not much could happen. You have to be emotional.

Maija: Now, a lot of the clubs I have seen, a lot of the comedians are no longer trying to become stand-ups because they are trying to develop their shows strictly for television.

Phyllis: You mean...

Maija: They get into it as a stepping stone. And, what they have done is push people to develop what is known as point of view comedy. Where a lot of them look to, like a Richard Pryor, which kind of changed... I think when Pryor started doing comedy, it changed comedy a little bit, where people tried, a lot of comics I know are trying to work directly out of themselves, out of their tragedies, out of pain.

Phyllis: Well, that is true of Christopher Titus. Even his show is his actual personal past life, recreated.

Maija:	Yeah.
Phyllis:	Well, all comedy rises out of tragedy.
Maija:	When you worked on your material, did you find things out of your personal life that were difficult to deal with, that you built material out of?
Phyllis:	Yes. Fortunately, I had already had neighbors and children and dogs and cats and cops and robbers. I had the whole thing. You see, someone like you, who is young and beautiful, I feel much empathy and I realize it's very difficult, more difficult for you to find things to bitch about because you haven't been maybe hurt or have enough history.
Maija:	It's a different life experience.
Phyllis:	When you think of your audience, it depends on the age group, of course. If they are terribly young, they will identify with you more easily and what it is that you are going to bitch about. Because comedy is mainly just bitching. Oh, this and that and what and what. Like I am right now I am listening to a new Richard Lewis CD, and he has this wonderful stance. Wonderful platform where he's sick. He is constantly in need of therapy and he has made it work. He wears all black. You know, he is the sick, sick, completely Jewish wreak. And it works, you see. And he does. Everything makes him nervous. And he is, you know, just ridden with guilt and, you see, in other words, everything he says now,

	works within that stance that he has created. Have you created a stance?
Maija:	I am trying to find it.
Phyllis:	You're still looking for it.
Maija:	Yeah, I am , I am.
Phyllis:	How long have you been working?
Maija:	Six years.
Phyllis:	Six years. Oh it takes a long time. Things develop. It's called evolution. In your case, your evolution. Oh God, when I think of the, there are so many things. Number one, simply, how do you get on? How do you say hello to an audience. Very important. Because it's your big chance to come out and grab. And if you don't, you are going to work harder trying to get them.
Maija:	Yeah.
Phyllis:	And that was one of my big problems. How to get on.
Maija:	What was the difficulty that you specifically had during that time? Is it being a woman by yourself?
Phyllis:	No, it wasn't that. It was just how to say "Hello" to each new audience.
Maija:	I think for me I understand the difficulty in

	bridging the gaps.
Phyllis:	Between what?
Maija:	Between the different audiences. Because I, when I first started, I tried to go directly into the trends.
Phyllis:	Trends?
Maija:	Like the trends of, like they had the hip-hop comedy, and then they had that it's a point of view, the tragic family comedy, and that becomes…
Phyllis:	And you actually talked about comedy?
Maija:	No, I actually went on and created almost different personas.
Phyllis:	For yourself.
Maija:	For myself and now I am split between…
Phyllis:	And where are you now?
Maija:	Split between which way to go.
Phyllis:	Between hip-hop and point of view.
Maija:	Point of view. I find that there is too many different, it's hard to find who I am in the middle of it. I'm just trying to find who I am in the middle of it.
Phyllis:	Well, you see, when you find out who you really

	are, who you want to be, the real you, then you are home.
Maija:	How long did it take you to find yourself?
Phyllis:	I had a director who was pointing me in the direction of being she-she. He kept taking me to female impersonators. To teach me. Please. He was making a female impersonator out of me. I am already a female, Lloyd, darling. I mean, please. I was dressing like a female, like a transvestite. I mean, there would have been a lot of questions. What is that? Hahahaha. And his material that he was helping me with was she-she, and I would never have made a good living. I would have been at a certain level of a cult sort of thing. I would have been right there. It's a wonderful question you asked because I haven't even given this deep thought to it. But it was extremely... I will never forget one day I was walking down the street and I said to him, "Why is it that when I come up with an idea, you veto it?" Because I was getting in the real me. The housewife, the cooking, the kids, you see what I mean? He was writing wonderful parodies for me, and I will say they were wonderful, but they were she-she. They were certainly not for the Grey Line tour. You know what that is?
Maija:	No, I don't.
Phyllis:	That's people from Iowa, Indiana, Montana and they come in this little night club. They're frightened out of their minds. Because they are in a basement and they lived on a farm.

And now here they are in San Francisco for the first time. And you see reaching those people, greatest thing that ever happened to me. Because that happened right at the very beginning. In other words, how to reach people who are aware of your experiences. So, you see, I reached them with what they knew about. Kids, animals, real life, real life. Bad experiences that go wrong like, cooking failures. Ha-ha. I had enough. I already have had enough to know that you can have a lot of trouble with cooking. The first custard pie I ever made, I was so proud of myself as a young housewife, you see, that was my career then. The custard pie developed a little water on the top and I thought, mm, just slide that off and then when I made it a little crooked, the whole custard thing fell out on the dress. There goes my pie. I had worked for hours. But this is the thing. When I started doing what I knew about and what I cared about, kids, neighbors, then is when I started my ascent to real progress. Then, of course, I got rid of Lloyd. Hahaha. He was talented, but he was pointing me in his direction. And I was right, but remember, it's your gut feeling.

Maija: Now what about if you are in a room and there is an audience member that becomes disruptive, and sometimes if you go on...

Phyllis: Hecklers.

Maija: Hecklers, and sometimes the blue comic that goes on before you.

Phyllis: Hard to follow.

Maija: And a woman comes on stage, and it's a rough room and there's a guy in the front and he becomes a little hostile and drunk and you have to, I guess, sometimes because if you can't shut him up, sometimes you have to come down to his level. How do you feel about that? In finding yourself, in having to come down to that level.

Phyllis: These are the things, you as a youth and working at a certain level, these places, where they don't have to pay a lot to get in, and they are, like I say, often drunk. Leave it to a drunk to think that he is, Charles de Gaulle, running a country. You know. They just get out of hand. It's a terrible problem and I, I just, I don't know, I don't know how to do that. I wouldn't know. I tell you what. I used to, when I had a few of those; I would ignore them and just keep working over them. Just keep going ahead louder than they were and just ignore them. I know there is another thing you can do. Have a light put on them. It just scares the crap out of them.

Maija: That's actually good.

Phyllis: Yeah. And tell them, "And if you want to work with me, lets light you up, like I am and lets work together." And boy do they shut up. Because they are in the dark. They are protected. That's one thing you might try. Because it's kind of fun. Hahaha. To destroy somebody.

Maija: Was it difficult for you working in a night club atmosphere, especially at the time you were working, when you first started?

Phyllis: Well, I always, fortunately, there was in those days, there was a very high brow circuit, where the people and the audience were very brainy. I don't know if there is a circuit like that. In Chicago it was Mr. Kelly's, in San Francisco there was two clubs, Hungry I, Purple Onion, in New York- Blue Angel, Bon Soir, Number One 5th Avenue. Now, I don't know whether we have comedy clubs, but I don't think they are at the level of those places.

Maija: No, they are not

Phyllis: No. I worked a few. But when I work them, it's my own group coming in, you see. It's not like going in to a regular night. One of those places.

Maija: Would you ever advise your daughter or a young woman to become a stand-up, if they say they want to become a stand-up comedian. Would you give them the advice to go in a different direction?

Phyllis: No. It's so rewarding

Maija: In what way?

Phyllis: Oh my God! Great power. You have an audience. They are yours to play with. And when you can make them laugh on cue, there's no thrill like it. And you can always be better. It's a no ceiling career where you can always become more artistic. Better. You can always be better. You can always have better material. You can always work constantly on material forever. And so, you know, there's no ceiling. So many jobs you complete them, they're through.

Maija: Working with Bob Hope. What was that like?

Phyllis: That was a great joy because he is certainly an authority on comedy, on classic comedy. He is a one liner king. I mean all his monologues were on the principle of one liners- setup, payoff, setup, payoff and he goes for 6 laughs a minute. It's like a science. He is more like a humor scientist. And in his position as such an important, whoever is, no one will ever, it won't be possible to top his experience because when you start in vaudeville and then radio and 60 years in television and 200 movies, a person has to live to be 400 to top that. It's just great fun.

Maija: You worked in a number of, you worked in three movies.

Phyllis: Three movies and they were, *Boy, Did I Get a*

Wrong Number, Eight On the Lam, and *The Private Navy of Sgt. O'Farrell.*

Maija: What was your favorite?

Phyllis: Well, the one they play all the time, the one with Elke Summer and Cesare A... What's his name...I don't know his name. Oh god! There are so many good people in that. *Boy, Did I Get a Wrong Number.* And Margie Lord played his wife and the detectives were two old character actors, who were just so wonderful. It had a great cast and the story was just adorable.

Maija: When you went into these, did you know they would become the greatest classics? Did you think.. When you walked into them...

Phyllis: I got to tell you a funny secret that shows how dumb I was. You know, Bob Hope was noted for being a cue card man. You could see him reading the cue cards. Looked right past the person reading. Didn't matter because he is so great and accepted by everyone for what he is. So, I assumed in the movie there would be cue cards...I never.. You know, *Splendor In the Grass* was eons before. And I was in the first scene of *Boy, Did I get A Wrong Number* and just before I went out to do the scene, found out that there were no cue cards, and I hadn't even read the scene. Holy! Talk about out on a limb. I was hanging by a twig. It was the fastest I ever learned anything in my life. So dumb! This is the way you learn by these terrible things that happen to you.

Maija: What is the most difficult experience you've ever had in show business?

Phyllis: My...there have been so many...I don't think you have time. And when you ask me the most difficult ever.. Oh, one time, a guy ... I had to come out in Chicago... and, you know how it is when you're working at the level with the audience on the floor...big, big ...ball room... whole bunch of people there for a benefit and then a guy came out at that level, and I had to follow him, and he did about 30 minutes on cancer. I think when I came out, everybody was still wiping away the tears. And I have one of the worst shows... Number one I was depressed.

Maija: Yeah ..yeah.. what a great way to go in and do the material..

Phyllis: I was so distraught.. I wouldn't even see friends after that show. I was so depressed and so destroyed. You know, you want to be funny. But there is no way that I could entertain that audience and I came off with a total failure. But only for that night, darling.

Maija: Well, it seems to change so much. It goes from.. You know, we got one night up and one night down.

Phyllis: Well, a lot of things are... Comedy is more susceptible to the physicality of a room and the people, the best room to work for comedy is red and round, thrust stage, raked seating. There's a room like that. It's the Sammy Davis room at Harrah's in Reno. It seats about 550. It's raked for the people. That means that every seat in the house has a perfect view of you. It's red. It's round, and it is a thrust stage, but it doesn't even need it. The room is so great. And everybody knows what they're doing. The sound people, the lighting people, they're all seasoned pros. Now, when you get something like that going for you, you come out ahead. There are times when...the worst room in the world to work for us is the ballrooms where it isn't meant to be a working room. They put boxes, you stand on the boxes. You may have a joint between two boxes where you catch your heel. The trick is to make them put a rug down, so you don't have to be aware of your feet. Look, I'm not an organ player. Please. But, you see, things get in your way. Oh, and those rooms...everybody is at a table of ten and that means half the room has their back to you, unless they want to turn around. And another thing, they aren't sitting close enough together. The ideal thing is when people are sitting all facing you and close to each other. These are the things that help you, and when you are up against rotten circumstances...say a light room, too much light. Comedy is so delicate, so

	delicate.
Maija:	Now, what is it like being a concert pianist?
Phyllis:	Oh, well that's a whole other story.
Maija:	In the middle of all of this, you decided to… continue your career in music
Phyllis:	It was an accident. I mean, everything that happened to me was an accident. The Pittsburgh people called from the symphony. They said, "We'd like you to do a Pops concert with the Pittsburgh Symphony." I hear the word symphony and I think, "Well, they must want some kind of music from me." They wanted my act. But then I said, "Oh, I'd be delighted." So, I wrote a whole music act just for that Pittsburgh Symphony.
Maija:	Really?

Phyllis:	Then it became ten years of a hundred symphonies in the USA and Canada. I wrote a whole hour with another character, no Fang. She was very grande, darling. Her name was Dame Illya Dillya. She came out dressed like the Queen of England. So, I did have a shot at

	some other kind of…you realize the symphony audience, that's a certain kind of audience.
Maija:	That's incredible that you could reach them.
Phyllis:	I could reach them because I had this background in classical music.

Maija:	How do you feel about people like a Jerry Lewis that had said at the Aspen festival…
Phyllis:	"There are no funny women."
Maija:	"There is no such thing as funny women."
Phyllis:	Well, he really put his foot in his mouth. I'll bet his foot is still covered with saliva. Haha. And he had to get out of it somehow. And it was so sweet of him to mention my name. He said, "Well, there's Phyllis Diller."
Maija:	He had to.
Phyllis:	He had to think of somebody quick. Really.
Maija:	Well, I have to say that it's such an honor.

	Thank you so much for the time, the advice and information. I'm honored even to meet you.
Phyllis:	Well, Maija, its so much fun to talk to somebody who understands the whole thing, and you certainly do.
Maija:	Thank you. Thank you very much. I really appreciate it.

Phyllis:	It was a terrific interview. That's a special talent. That's a very special talent. You're very good. That's very difficult to do. I know. I know. I gotta go.
Maija:	Thank you so much.

Thank You Phyllis

www.ingramcontent.com/pod-product-compliance
Lightning Source LLC
Chambersburg PA
CBHW041820040426

42452CB00004B/161